IS STEM EVERYWHERE

JOHN LESLEY

LIGHT

RAINBOWS AND LASERS

THE SCIENCE OF LIGHT

REDBACK
publishing

Redback Publishing
PO Box 357 Frenchs Forest NSW 2086
Australia

www.redbackpublishing.com
orders@redbackpublishing.com

ISBN 978-1-922322-60-9

Author: John Lesley
Editor: Marlene Vaughan
Designer: Redback Publishing

Original illustrations © Redback Publishing 2021
Originated by Redback Publishing

Printed and bound in China

Acknowledgements
Abbreviations: l—left, r—right, b—bottom, t—top, c—centre, m—middle
We would like to thank the following for permission to reproduce photographs: (Images © shutterstock)
p28tl By Nicole Glass Photography.

MIX
Paper from
responsible sources
FSC® C020056
www.fsc.org

A catalogue record for this book is available from the National Library of Australia

CONTENTS

LIGHT

Our sense of sight depends on light, but what is light? Is it something solid? Where does it come from? Find out the answers to all these questions in the following chapters.

People are not the only living things that respond to light. Plants react to light too. There are even some chemicals that change in the presence of light.

We can see distant objects in the Universe because light from them has travelled through space. In our own skies on Earth, light creates rainbows, the auroras at the poles, and even the blue sky.

Many inventions use light, including telescopes, microscopes and lasers.

The creation of light sources to dispel the darkness at night has been one of the factors that have helped in the development of civilisations. Being able to continue working or socialising at night has extended the time we have to learn, invent, read and enjoy the company of our friends and families.

Sources of light, whether they are the Sun, fire, oil lamps, candles, lasers or electric lighting are vital to all human societies.

NIGHT AND DAY

NIGHT AND DAY

We are so used to night and day on Earth that we hardly ever think about what causes this difference in lighting.

The Earth spins around about once every 24 hours. As it turns, only half of it faces the Sun and receives light. This is daytime. The side of the Earth that is turned away from the Sun experiences night.

EARTH ROTATION: 24 HOURS

OUR MOON

At night, we receive some light from the Moon and stars. The Moon reflects light from the Sun, and does not produce its own light. As the Moon revolves around the Earth, it seems to change shape because only some parts of it are illuminated by the Sun. These are the only parts we can see, resulting in a full, half or crescent Moon in the sky.

MOON ROTATION: 28 DAYS

MOON ORBITS EARTH: 28 DAYS

EARTH ORBITS THE SUN: 365 DAYS

DUSK AND DAWN

Between night and day there is a short time when the light is halfway between dark and light. We call this dawn in the morning and dusk, or twilight, at night. During these periods, the Sun is not fully facing the Earth, so only some of the light from it reaches us.

SUN
ROTATION:
21 DAYS

WHAT MAKES THE SKY BLUE?

Light from the Sun is scattered by the gases in the atmosphere. The blue light gets scattered more than any other colour, and this is why we see a blue sky.

OUR SUN

The Sun is our main source of light. The Sun is a star and, if we could see it from far away in space, it would look like any other star in our galaxy.

AIR
MOLECULES
SCATTER
BLUE LIGHT

ATMOSPHERE

SOLAR ECLIPSES

In ancient times, people were terrified of eclipses. They thought that the disappearance of the Sun's light during the daytime meant that something very bad was about to happen.

Eclipses can now be predicted with great accuracy because we know the way the Earth revolves around the Sun, and the Moon revolves around the Earth. When the Sun is covered during the day in an eclipse, it is because the Moon has moved in front of it.

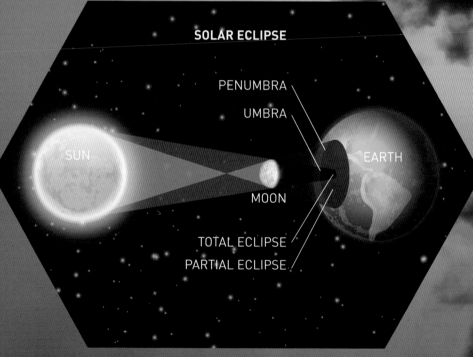

SOLAR ECLIPSE

PENUMBRA
UMBRA
SUN
EARTH
MOON
TOTAL ECLIPSE
PARTIAL ECLIPSE

HOW CAN THE LITTLE MOON BLOCK OUT THE HUGE SUN?

It is just by chance that we are living at a time when the Moon is at a distance from the Earth that allows it to block out the

At some time in the far distant future, the Moon will move further away and appear smaller. It will then no longer be able to

LUNAR ECLIPSES

An eclipse of the Moon happens when the Earth moves between the Sun and the Moon. The Earth's shadow then covers the Moon, stopping it reflecting any sunlight back onto Earth.

LUNAR ECLIPSE

UMBRA

SUN   EARTH   MOON

PENUMBRA

BEWARE

Do not look directly at an eclipse of the Sun. Even the small amount of light that begins to show around the edges can damage your eyes. Looking directly at the Sun can lead to blindness.

HOW DOES LIGHT GET FROM ONE PLACE TO ANOTHER?

Even though the Sun is millions of miles away, the light it produces takes only about 8 minutes to reach us on Earth.

Nothing in the Universe can travel faster than light. Its speed is 300,000 kilometres per second. This sounds very fast but the Universe is so huge that light takes an incredibly long time to get across our own Milky Way galaxy from one end to the other.

Light mostly travels in straight lines here on Earth, but it can behave very strangely in outer space. Gravity can bend light, making it move in a curve. As light moves near a massive body, like a planet, a galaxy or the weirdest stuff of all, dark matter, the gravity can pull light off its straight course.

ACTUAL DIRECTION TO STAR

APPARENT DIRECTION TO STAR

10

CROOKES RADIOMETER

THE LIGHT MILL

Crookes radiometer is an invention that shows how the energy of light can be changed into movement. Inside a glass container, black and white panels are positioned on a post so that they can spin. As light hits the black panel, the panels start to spin around.

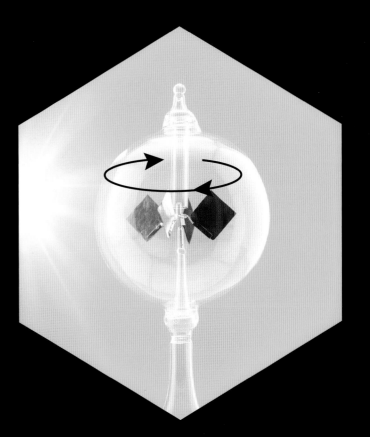

WHAT IS LIGHT MADE OF?

Light is electromagnetic energy. It can travel as a wave of energy, or it can also exist as a photon, which is a particle that has no mass. This idea about the double nature of light is so unusual that scientists continue to study the behaviour of photons and light waves.

ELECTROMAGNETIC ENERGY

PHOTONS

LET THE LIGHT IN!

WHEN LIGHT STRIKES AN OBJECT, THREE THINGS CAN HAPPEN:

1 TRANSPARENT OBJECT

The light passes straight through and we can clearly see what is on the other side of the object.

Examples - clear glass, clear plastics, clear water

2 TRANSLUCENT OBJECT

Some of the light passes through, but as it does so it is scattered in many directions, causing objects on the other side to appear fuzzy.

Examples - some plastics, frosted glass used in bathrooms, sheer fabrics used for clothes and curtains

3 OPAQUE OBJECT

None of the light gets through, causing the object to cast a shadow.

Examples - people, cars, wood, some plastics

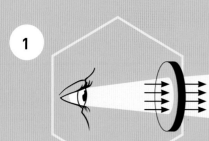

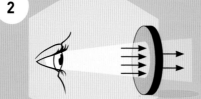

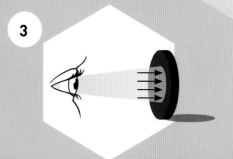

HOW WE USE SHADOWS

The ability of an opaque object to cast a shadow is something living things use to survive and to make their lives easier.

Shadows provide people and animals with shelter from strong sunlight

People use the shadow on a sundial to tell the time

In rainforests, delicate plants grow in the shadow of the big trees

Umbrellas at the beach shade us from too much sunlight

Shadow puppets provide amusement

REFLECTION

MIRRORS

When light strikes a mirror, it is reflected straight back to the viewer. This is the light that lets us see ourselves in a mirror, or in the shiny surface of a metal frying pan.

BRICK WALLS

Objects that are not shiny have a rough surface. Sometimes this roughness is microscopic, but it is still enough to make light reflect off these types of surfaces at lots of different angles.

This is what stops us being able to see our reflection in a brick wall.

NO REFLECTIONS

When no light is being bounced or reflected off an object, then we cannot see it. This is why we cannot see furniture in the dark, and bump into it if we try to walk around a dark room. It is also why we find it hard to see a clean, glass door, or the surface of still water. In these situations, very little light is reflected off the smooth surfaces.

Q: How can we sometimes see ourselves in a glass window, but at other times we can only see straight through it?

A: Although a glass window is mostly transparent, a small amount of light is still reflected back off its smooth surface. When one side is very bright, and the other side is darker, the person on the bright side can see the reflected light more easily, and the window becomes a mirror.

REFRACTION

The refraction of light as it passes through different transparent substances is used by people to create technological devices. Microscopes, reading glasses, telescopes and contact lenses all depend on the refraction of light.

When light enters some transparent materials, such as water, it bends. This is why the bottom of a swimming pool looks closer to you than it really is. It's also why a straw in a glass of water looks bent.

Jewellery makers use the refraction of light through crystals, such as diamonds, to make beautiful pieces for people to wear.

Our own eyes contain a natural lens that refracts light as it passes through it, enabling us to see things clearly.

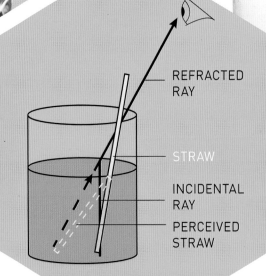

REFRACTED RAY

STRAW

INCIDENTAL RAY

PERCEIVED STRAW

MIRAGES ON HOT ROADS

Refraction of light does not only occur when it enters a clear liquid or a solid. Layers of air at different temperatures can also cause the refraction of light as it moves from one layer to another. The unusual effect this causes is called a mirage.

A common mirage is a hot road that can appear to have water over its surface in the distance. As light enters the layer of air that has been heated up through contact with the hot bitumen of the road, the light refracts or bends. Our eyes see this as a shimmering reflection of the sky, which looks like it is water over the ground.

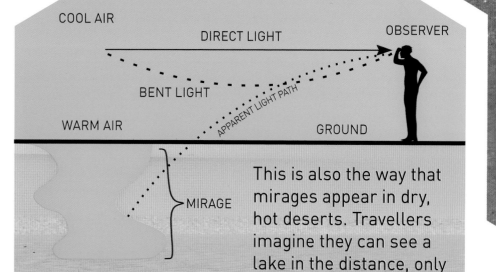

COOL AIR

DIRECT LIGHT

OBSERVER

BENT LIGHT

APPARENT LIGHT PATH

WARM AIR

GROUND

MIRAGE

This is also the way that mirages appear in dry, hot deserts. Travellers imagine they can see a lake in the distance, only to find dry sand when they finally reach it.

WHAT WOULD WE DO WITHOUT LENSES?

Without lenses, we would not be able to see clearly, we could not observe tiny microorganisms and we could not marvel at the sight of galaxies far beyond our own.

A lens is a transparent object that has a curve. As light enters the object, it is refracted, or bent. It is this bending of the light that makes things seem bigger or smaller when we see them through a lens.

CAMERAS

Cameras use lenses to direct the light that comes into them. They may have a group of convex and concave lenses in them.

UNEXPECTED LENSES

If you look through a glass or plastic bottle as you slowly move it around, you may see that things appear magnified. This happens because the curve of the bottle is acting as a lens. Look through the side of a light globe and you will see reality distorted by the light bending as it passes through the curved surfaces.

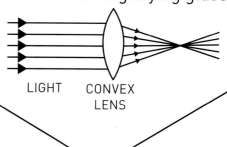

CONCAVE LENS

A concave lens is curved inwards, making it thinner in the middle part than towards it edges. As the straight lines of light from an object enter the lens, they are bent outwards. Concave lenses used in security peepholes on doors allow us to see a wide view of everything outside.

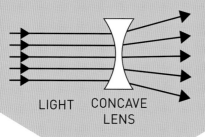

LIGHT   CONCAVE
         LENS

CONVEX LENS

A convex lens is curved outwards, making it thicker in the middle part than towards it edges. As the straight lines of light from an object enter the lens, they are bent together. This makes the object appear closer to us and therefore bigger or magnified, as through a microscope, binoculars or a magnifying glass.

LIGHT   CONVEX
         LENS

EYES AND LIGHT

Human eyes are complex structures that gather light and send signals to the brain, telling us what information the light is carrying about our surroundings. This is how we see.

Some animals do not have eyes that can see details. Instead, they can only respond to light and dark. Earthworms can sense when they are in the light by using light sensitive spots called photoreceptors on their bodies.

In contrast to the earthworm, there are some animals whose eyes are much better than ours. One example is the eagle, whose eyes allow them to see details a whole kilometre away.

PINHOLE CAMERAS AND EYES

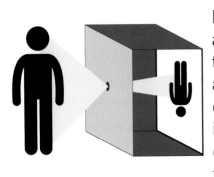

In a pinhole camera, a box allows light to enter through a tiny pinhole. This light creates an upside-down image on the opposite side of the box. This is because the light rays from outside cross over as they go through the pinhole.

Our eyes act like pinhole cameras as light enters them. The upside-down images formed are sent to the brain, but we know to turn them around in our mind so that what we see is the correct way up.

THE PARTS OF OUR EYES

PUPIL

The pupil is the hole in the middle of the circular iris. The iris responds to too much light by closing the pupil down to a small hole. In a dimly lit area, the pupil will open wider to let more light in.

The reason it takes a while for us to be able to see clearly if we go from sunlight to a room inside is that it takes a little while for our pupils to open wide enough to let enough light in so that we can see.

In a pet cat's eyes the pupils are vertical slits in bright light. In low light a cat's pupils open up to round shapes, like ours.

IRIS

This is the part of our eyes that makes them blue, brown or green.

LENS

Behind the pupil is a convex lens. It focuses the light coming into the eye so that we see a sharp image. Unlike the glass lens in a microscope, the lens in an eye can change shape.

OPTIC NERVE

At the back of our eye is the optic nerve. This responds to the light by sending a message to our brain. The brain then processes the message and tells us what we are looking at.

RAINBOWS AND PRISMS

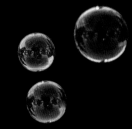

The light from the Sun or from an electric light globe seems to have no colour. Because of this, we call it white light.

White light is actually made up of many different colours all mixed together. We can see what these colours are when the light is bent through a prism. As this happens, the light separates into the rainbow colours. All these colours together are called the visible spectrum. Colours of the spectrum are always arranged in the same order.

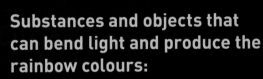

Substances and objects that can bend light and produce the rainbow colours:
- some carefully sliced crystals, such as diamonds
- soap bubbles
- pyramid-shaped piece of glass, called a prism
- water droplets
- shiny side of a CD

HOW RAINBOWS FORM

After rain, when there are billions of tiny water droplets in the air, the sunlight shining through each drop is split into rainbow colours. A rainbow is always on the side of the sky which is opposite from where the Sun is located.

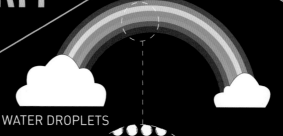

WATER DROPLETS

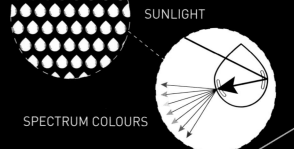

SUNLIGHT

SPECTRUM COLOURS

MAKE YOUR OWN RAINBOW

Try making your own rainbow on a sunny day. Spray water from a hose or spray bottle so that it forms tiny droplets in the air. You might be able to see your very own rainbow.

THE VISIBLE SPECTRUM COLOURS

| ULTRA-VIOLET | VIOLET | BLUE | GREEN | YELLOW | ORANGE | RED | INFRARED |

HAVE YOU EVER WONDERED WHAT CAUSES THINGS TO HAVE DIFFERENT COLOURS?

Colour is a characteristic of the type of light reflected from an object. When we say that an object is opaque, and absorbs light, we really mean that it absorbs most of the rainbow colours of light, and only reflects back at us the light of its surface colour.

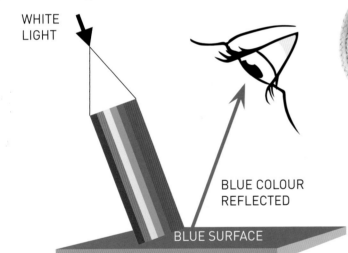

WHITE LIGHT

BLUE COLOUR REFLECTED

BLUE SURFACE

If ordinary, white light from the Sun is falling on an opaque object, like a blue hat, we see it as blue because the hat is reflecting the blue light back at us, but absorbing all the other colours.

WHAT ABOUT BLACK AND WHITE?

If an object looks white, this is because it is reflecting all the colours back at us. If an object looks black, it is absorbing all the light. Black is not really a colour, but an absence of colour. Because black objects absorb all the light that falls on them, black things get hotter in sunlight than white things, which reflect nearly all the light. Test this for yourself by putting on a black top and then a white top when you are standing in the sunlight. You will feel much hotter in the black top.

HOW TV SCREENS MAKE COLOUR

An LCD television screen is made of thousands of tiny dots in the three basic colours of light – red, green and blue. As each tiny dot is turned on or off, and the light from them is mixed, we see the whole range of colours.

PRIMARY COLOURS

Primary colours are basic colours that can be mixed together to make every other colour. The basic colours of light are different from the basic colours we use when mixing paints to paint a picture.

3 BASIC COLOURS OF LIGHT

3 BASIC COLOURS OF PAINT

LASERS

Lasers produce light of only one colour. Unlike the Sun's light, which will split into rainbow colours when it passes through a prism, laser light will not be able to split, as it is only one colour. Laser light can be concentrated, making it very powerful. When the light from a strong laser hits a surface, it creates a large amount of heat at a tiny point. This heat is so high it can melt metal.

DANGER

Lasers are dangerous because their light is so strong. Never look directly at a laser light.

MANUFACTURING

Laser cutters of various strengths are used in manufacturing to cut all sorts of substances, from fabrics to wood and plastic.

EDUCATION

A low-power, hand-held laser light can be used as a pointer on a screen during a lecture.

ELECTRON

PHOTON

100% REFLECTIVE MIRROR

95% REFLECTIVE MIRROR

LASER BEAM

ATOM

QUARTZ FLASH TUBE

LASERS IN MEDICINE

A laser beam is used in surgery to make very precise cuts. Since it is so hot, the tiny beam can also reduce bleeding by sealing blood vessels as it cuts through them.

LASERS FOR MEASUREMENT

By measuring the time taken for a beam of laser light to strike an object, we can work out how far away the object is. The Apollo astronauts who went to the Moon in 1969 left a mirror on its surface. Back on Earth, scientists shone a laser beam at the mirror and measured how long it took for the beam to be reflected and to arrive back on Earth. They could then work out a very accurate figure for the distance between the Moon and the Earth.

TECHNOLOGY USING LIGHT

BINOCULARS

STROBE LIGHT

SUNGLASSES

CONTACT LENSES

CAMERA

Canon

EOS

TORCH

LED TV SCREEN

HOLOGRAPHIC IMAGE

TELESCOPE

OIL LAMP

MAGNIFYING GLASS

SOLAR MIRROR

LIGHT SPECTROMETER

SPECTACLES

SHOW LIGHT

FLUORESCENT TUBE

CANDLE

KALEIDOSCOPE

VIDEO RECORDER

MOVIE PROJECTOR

MICROSCOPE

PERISCOPE

STAINED GLASS WINDOWS

GAS LAMP

29

INVISIBILITY

Human eyes struggle to see an object when light goes straight through it. This happens when the object is very transparent.

A transparent glass wall or door needs small stickers placed on it so that people can see it easily. Otherwise, since most of the light goes straight through it, the glass becomes invisible and people may walk into it.

Black holes in space are things that absorb light and let none back out. Astronomers cannot see the black hole, but they can see what is around it.

IS IT POSSIBLE TO BECOME INVISIBLE?

Fantasy stories often have invisibility as a part of the plot. But is this really possible or not?

If an object were invisible, it would not send any light to an onlooker's eyes. In a dark place, where there is no light, everything is invisible.
Some black objects absorb most of the light that falls on them. If we were able to make the surface completely light absorbent, so that no light was reflected, then we would not be able to see the object. Scientists are working on this possibility.

WORDS ABOUT LIGHT

aurora — colourful bands of light that appear in the sky near the north and south poles of the Earth

black — colour that is the absence of reflected light

dark matter — material that exists in space but which is currently a mystery

dusk — period of the day just before sunset

eclipse — one planet blocking the sunlight from another

electromagnetism — one of the basic forces in the Universe

focus — making something appear in sharp detail

LCD screen — liquid crystal display screen

microscopic — too tiny to be seen without the use of a microscope

mirage — illusion caused by light encountering hot air near the ground

opacity — ability of a material to absorb light and cast a shadow

optic nerve — nerve that carries visual information from the eyes to the brain

periscope — machine used to see around corners by reflecting light from mirrors

photon — weightless particle of energy that forms light

photoreceptor — sensory device or organ that responds to light

primary colour — colour that can be mixed with others to make every other known colour

speed of light — about 300,000 kilometres per second

strobe light — device used to make flashes of light at regular intervals

visible spectrum — electromagnetic radiation that can be seen by the human eye

white light — mixture of all colours of light

INDEX